P9-CAL-676

10-3-201

Yumi Hotta

Oftentimes I have trouble with story-boards. When that happens, I just keep telling myself, "It's okay, Obata Sensei will think of something!"
—Yumi Hotta

t all began when Yumi Hotta played a pick-up game of Go with her father-in-law. As she was learning how to play, Ms. Hotta thought it might be fun to create a story around the traditional board game. More confident in her storytelling abilities than her drawing skills, she submitted the beginnings of **Hikaru no Go** to **Weekly Shonen Jump**'s Story King Award. The Story King Award is an award that picks the best story, manga, character design and youth (under 15) manga submissions every year in Japan. As fate would have it, Ms. Hotta's story (originally named, "**Kokonotsu no Hoshi**"), was a runner-up in the "Story" category of the Story King Award. Many years earlier, Takeshi Obata was a runner-up for the Tezuka Award, another Japanese manga contest sponsored by **Weekly Shonen Jump** and **Monthly Shonen Jump**. An editor assigned to Mr. Obata's artwork came upon Ms. Hotta's story and paired the two for a full-fledged manga about Go. The rest is modern Go history.

HIKARU NO GO VOL. 1
SHONEN JUMP Manga Edition

This graphic novel contains material that was originally published in English from
SHONEN JUMP #13 to #16.

STORY BY YUMI HOTTA
ART BY TAKESHI OBATA
Supervised by YUKARI UMEZAWA (5 Dan)

Translation & English Adaptation/Andy Nakatani
Touch-Up Art & Lettering/Adam Symons
Lettering Assistants/Josh Simpson, Walden Wong
Cover & Graphics Design/Sean Lee
Editor/Livia Ching

Printed in the U.S.A.

Published by VIZ Media, LLC
P.O. Box 77010
San Francisco, CA 94107

11
First printing, May 2004
Eleventh printing, October 2016

www.viz.com

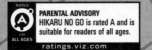

PARENTAL ADVISORY
HIKARU NO GO is rated A and is
suitable for readers of all ages.
ratings.viz.com

THE WORLD'S
MOST POPULAR MANGA
SHONEN JUMP
www.shonenjump.com

①

DESCENT OF THE GO MASTER

STORY BY **YUMI HOTTA**
ART BY **TAKESHI OBATA**
Supervised by **YUKARI UMEZAWA (5 Dan)**

CONTENTS

GAME 1
"Descent of the Go Maste

UMF...

HEY, LOOK AT THAT...

DON'T BE DUMB. THIS IS A GO BOARD.

A FIVE-IN-A-ROW BOARD.

BET I'LL GET A LOT OF MONEY FOR IT! ANTIQUES ARE POPULAR THESE DAYS, YOU KNOW.

AND IT SURE DOES LOOK OLD. GRANDPA MUST'VE USED IT A LONG TIME AGO.

BESIDES, I NEED THE MONEY. MY PARENTS CUT OFF MY ALLOWANCE 'CAUSE I ONLY GOT 8 POINTS ON THAT SOCIAL STUDIES TEST.

DON'T WORRY!

WIPE WIPE

ARE YOU SURE IT'S ALL RIGHT? I MEAN, MAYBE YOU SHOULD ASK--

8

DARNIT! WHY WON'T THIS STAIN COME OUT?

NO, IT'S NOT!

BUT HIKARU, IT'S PERFECTLY CLEAN.

?

8 points...

WHY DIDN'T YOU STUDY?

RIGHT HERE!!

HERE!

WHERE!?

WHERE?

LOOK, RIGHT HERE! LOOKS LIKE AN OLD BLOOD STAIN OR SOMETHING...

THAT'S WHAT I'VE BEEN TRYING TO TELL YOU!

You can see it?

HUH?

You can... hear my voice?

9

I JUST DON'T SEE ANYTHING, HIKARU...

You can really hear what I am saying?

.....

WHO'S THERE?! GRANDPA, IS THAT YOU? STOP PLAYING GAMES AND COME OUT!

AKARI, SOME-ONE'S UP HERE...

At long last...

At last...

YOU'RE FREAK-ING ME OUT.

STOP IT, HIKARU!

GULP

SHUF

To the gods, I offer my gratitude...

Hmm... Questions about history!

GASP!

I FEEL SO GROGGY. I GUESS IT'S LEFT OVER FROM WHAT HAPPENED YESTERDAY...

HOW CAN I TAKE A TEST IN *THIS* CONDITION?

IS THERE A PROBLEM, HIKARU?

....

I TOLD YOU NOT TO COME OUT!!

GRRR!

AND AN AMBU-LANCE TOOK HIM TO THE HOSPITAL.

HE FAINTED YESTER-DAY...

HIKARU'S NOT FEELING WELL TODAY...

UMM... EXCUSE ME...

IT'S ALL YOUR FAULT!

OKAY, EVERY- ONE! BACK TO YOUR SEATS!

KLATTA-SKOOT

YOU GOT TO RIDE IN AN AMBU- LANCE?!

NO WAY!

THAT'S SO COOL!

SO...

WHAT'S YOUR NAME, ANYWAY?

I am Fujiwara- no-Sai.

WEIRD NAME...

WHAT'S YOUR STORY?

I *TOLD* YOU, DON'T TALK TO ME UNLESS I TALK TO YOU FIRST!

MY CONSCIOUS- NESS IS *MINE*! I'M NOT GOING TO LET YOU HAVE IT!

GOT IT?!

Yes...

BAM

But, I was only trying to--

During the Heian Period*, I held a position in the Capital as Go instructor to the Emperor.

*Heian Period: 794-1185

HEIAN PERIOD...?

GO INSTRUCTOR?!

One day, he approached the Emperor with a suggestion...

In addition to myself, there was one other Go instructor.

It was such a happy time for me, I was able to play Go every day...

SO, WHO WON THE GAME?

I SEE...

Let us play a game to decide who shall keep his position.

Sir, I believe that you have need for only one Go instructor.

Everyone's attention was drawn to the board, it was only by mere chance that I saw it...

The game was dead even...

A single white stone lay in my opponent's Go bowl.*

*A container used to keep a player's stones

18

He waited for an opportune moment...

This, of course, has nothing to do with game play. A player need just explain the situation and return the misplaced stone to his opponent's Go bowl. However, *that* scoundrel...

To have one of your opponent's stones mixed in with your own is highly unusual, but on occasion, it *has* been known to happen.

...and then he placed the stone in with his prisoners...

YOU MEAN, HE CHEATED?!

!

YOU SCOUND-REL!

And just when I was about to call him on his foul--

I SAW WHAT YOU JUST DID! YOU PUT AN EXTRA BLACK STONE IN WITH YOUR PRISONERS!

FWISH

EVERYONE ELSE WAS LOOKING AT THE BOARD, BUT I SAW WHAT YOU DID! YOU HAD ONE OF *MY* STONES IN YOUR GO BOWL AND YOU SLIPPED IT IN WITH YOUR PRISONERS!

I SAW YOU!

WHAT?!

20

MMBLE

MMBLE

HAH! A PITIFUL EXCUSE!!

WH-WHAT ARE YOU SAYING?! THAT IS WHAT YOU JUST DID WITH A WHITE STONE!!

I REFUSE TO BELIEVE THAT EITHER OF YOU WOULD COMMIT SUCH AN UGLY OFFENSE IN MY PRESENCE.

NOW, ON WITH THE GAME!

SILENCE! ENOUGH!

.....

Upset with the turn of events, I was unable to calm myself down...

ON WITH THE GAME, INDEED...

HEH HEH...

...I lost the game...

Would my soul be allowed to depart this life and enter nirvana?

No...

My yearnings were strong, I wanted to play more Go...

To add insult to injury, my reputation was irreparably tarnished... I was banished from the Capital for my alleged treachery. With no other skills, no way or reason to live, two days later, I threw myself into the river...

.....

The child eventually became the best Go player of the Edo period.*

Unfortunately, he died a feeble and sickly death at the young age of 34.

*Edo Period: 1600-1868

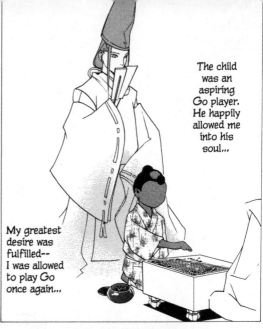

The child was an aspiring Go player. He happily allowed me into his soul...

My greatest desire was fulfilled-- I was allowed to play Go once again...

HON'INBO-SHUSAKU, HUH?

NEVER HEARD OF HIM... SO, THE BLOOD STAINS ON THAT GO BOARD MUST'VE BEEN FROM HIM...

He was a very good person...

His name was Hon'inbo-Shusaku...

I still have not accomplished my goal...

Yes...

I SUPPOSE THAT MEANS YOU STILL WANT TO PLAY GO?

SINCE YOU'VE COME BACK TO THE REAL WORLD THROUGH ME...

26

SPLURP!

UGHH...

Nothing! I didn't do anything!

WHAT'D YOU DO TO ME?!

gasp

SPloroP!

huf

huf

HIKARU! ARE YOU OKAY?!

.....

MAYBE YOU SHOULD GO SEE THE SCHOOL NURSE.

I-I THINK I'M OKAY.

ARE YOU OKAY, HIKARU?

You must have felt my intense sorrow when I heard that I would be unable to play Go.

BUT THAT'S YOUR PROBLEM. I HAVE MY OWN PLANS *AND THEY DON'T INCLUDE GO!*

humph!

I CAN'T STOMACH THE THOU-SAND YEARS OF SADNESS YOU HAD BOTTLED UP.

huf

huf

WHOA!

HIKARU! EWW!!

BLECH!

ZUBLOSRCH!!

U G H H...

blah...

BLARGH

SOMEONE TAKE HIKARU TO SEE THE NURSE, NOW!!

HIKARU, PULL YOUR-SELF TOGE-THER!

GET AWAY FROM ME, HIKARU!

28

GASP.

GRRR!!

.....

.....

GLARE!

Gasp! ♡

OKAY, YOU WIN... I'LL PLAY GO OR WHATEVER YOU WANT...

fwump...

GLORP--!

Yes!

Okay!

LET ME JUST REMIND YOU, MY CONSCIOUS-NESS BELONGS ONLY TO ME!

SO, DON'T TALK TO ME, UNLESS I TALK TO YOU FIRST.

I GUESS IT WON'T HURT TO PLAY EVERY ONCE IN A WHILE...

IT'S BETTER THAN BEING KILLED OFF BY THIS VENGEFUL SPIRIT...

sigh...

29

THIS GUY, HE JUST MIGHT COME IN HANDY...

WAIT A MINUTE...

AND WHEN I BEAT HIM, HE'LL HAVE TO PAY UP!

I GOT IT! I'LL CHALLENGE GRANDPA TO A GAME!

YEAH, I FEEL FINE NOW! ♡

ARE YOU SURE, YOU'RE OKAY, HIKARU?

HIKARU...

HIKARU BARFED ON ME!

glop

I *TOLD* YOU NOT TO TALK TO ME!!

GRRR!!

?!

Your grandfather plays?! Is he good?!

30

HIKARU! YOU FEELING BETTER NOW?

I'M ALL BETTER NOW! SEE?

YOU SURE DID GIVE ME A SCARE!

I WAS SO SHOCKED WHEN AKARI CAME DOWN AND SAID YOU HAD PASSED OUT!

flex!

WANNA PLAY? WINNER GETS A THOUSAND YEN!*

I'M LEARNING HOW TO PLAY GO!

*APPROXIMATELY US$8.50

31

HEH HEH HEH... ACTUALLY...

SO, WHAT'S GOING ON IF YOU CAN'T TO SEE GRANDMA SHE'S OUT SHOPPING

YOU'RE LEARNING HOW TO PLAY GO?!

REALLY?!

♡GO?!

I'M AT GRANDPA'S...

...IT'S ME...

MOM...?

YEAH, I WON'T STAY TOO LONG...

OKAY...

OKAY, YOU JUST WAIT HERE! I'LL GO GET THE BOARD!

TUMP

TUMP

I'M GONNA USE THE PHONE, GRANDPA...

SAI! I TOLD YOU NOT TO TALK TO ME, UNLESS I TALK TO YOU FIRST!!

But, we should play more than just one game!

ONE GAME'S ENOUGH FOR NOW, GRANDPA...

Chak...

Heh heh heh!

SO YOU'VE FINALLY COME TO APPRECIATE THE FINER POINTS OF GO!

I'LL PLAY YOU AS MUCH AS YOU WANT!

OOPS!

DON'T WORRY ABOUT IT, GRANDPA, IT'S NOTHING!

I WAS JUST-- UH...I HAD A FIGHT WITH A FRIEND, AND I WAS JUST THINKING ABOUT HIM AND I, UH--

GRANDPA! I WASN'T TALKING TO *YOU!*

HEH HEH HEH! LET ME WARN YOU, I'M PRETTY GOOD!

GLINT

YOU SAID A THOUSAND YEN, RIGHT?

OKAY! LET'S START PLAYING!

GO AHEAD, PUT DOWN AS MANY STONES AS YOU WANT.

PUT DOWN STONES...?

FWUMP

WHAT'S THAT MEAN...?

A weaker player may place down stones on the board to create a more even match.

OH, IT'S LIKE A HANDICAP!

SEE FOR YOURSELF!!

TA-DA!

WOW!

GRANDPA, ARE YOU *REALLY* THAT GOOD?!

Hmph!

!

SAI, CAN YOU BEAT HIM?

I'm not sure... But, I think I can...

THE TALENTED HAWK KEEPS HIS TALONS HIDDEN! HEH HEH HEH!

NO WAY! I DIDN'T KNOW YOU WERE *THIS* GOOD!

FIRST PLACE IN THE TOWN GO TOURNAMENT?!

C'MON, NOW HIKARU. YOU'RE JUST BEING HEAD-STRONG.

BUT YOU JUST STARTED LEARNING HOW TO PLAY...

LET'S JUST PLAY. I *KNOW* I'M GOOD!

FORGET THE HANDICAP!

LET'S START PLAYING.

BUT, THAT'S FINE. YOU DON'T HAVE TO PUT DOWN ANY STONES.

ARE YOU SURE YOU KNOW HOW TO PLAY?

HIKARU! *BLACK* ALWAYS GOES FIRST!

I'M GOING TO BE WHITE!

Kshk

I LIKE THESE WHITE STONES!

?

sniff

.....

Kshk
Kshk

FINE, YOU GO FIRST, GRANDPA.

SAI...

.....

YOU'RE GETTING SO EMOTIONAL...

CAN'T BLAME YOU, THOUGH. YOU'VE BEEN WAITING OVER 140 YEARS TO PLAY...

I GUESS IT'S NOT GOING TO HURT TO LET YOU PLAY EVERY ONCE IN A WHILE...

Yes!

UMM... SAI?

KLAK

OKAY HIKARU, HERE WE GO...

They are called "Star Points."

A star point... on the first move...

Look at the board. There are nine points marked by black dots.

NINE BLACK DOTS...

STAR POINT?

The game must have advanced quite a bit in the past 140 years...

Hmm...

In Shusaku's time, it was unheard of to play an opening move on a star point.

WHAT'S WRONG HIKARU? HURRY UP AND MAKE YOUR MOVE!

UH-OH...

DARN! SAI HASN'T PLAYED IN 140 YEARS!

HE MIGHT'VE BEEN A GOOD PLAYER BACK IN THE EDO PERIOD, BUT CAN HE HOLD UP AGAINST A PLAYER FROM *MODERN* TIMES?!

ONE POINT BELOW WHAT?! WHERE?!

It's one point directly below the lower right star point.

THE 3-4 POINT? WHAT'S THAT?!

The 3-4 point in the lower right corner...

WHERE IN THE UPPER RIGHT CORNER?!

Next, play the upper right corner.

HURRY IT UP A BIT...

KLAK!

HERE...?

TNK

YOU'RE TAKING TOO MUCH TIME...

KLK!

...ABOVE THE STAR POINT... UM... HERE?

TNK

Play the 3-4 point. This time, above the star point.

THAT SETTLES IT. I'M NEVER PLAYING AGAIN!!

I DON'T EVEN KNOW THE FIRST THING ABOUT GO!

I'M SORRY...

I COULDN'T HELP IT...

BUT, YOU KNOW...

GLORP...!

FWUMP

YOUR MOOD SWINGS ARE AFFECTING ME TOO!

But, you said--

STOP GETTING SO DE-PRESSED!

40

YOU WOULDN'T HAPPEN TO KNOW ANYTHING ABOUT THE TEMPO REFORM, WOULD YOU?

I'VE GOT TO MAKE ALL THESE CORRECTIONS TO MY SOCIAL STUDIES TEST BY TOMORROW.

I'M THE ONE THAT SHOULD BE CRYING!

.....

The reforms included restriction of the movement of villagers to the cities as well as various other financial reforms...

The Tempo Reform...? Ah, yes... Senior Councilor Mizuno-Tadakuni.

WHAT DO YOU KNOW, SAI? YOU MIGHT BE OF SOME USE TO ME, AFTER ALL...

GOT IT-- URAGA BAY...

OKAY, THANKS. THAT'S ENOUGH.

Once, while I was visiting the castle, he--

He came into Uraga Bay with four warships...

WHERE DID PERRY SAIL INTO?

41

Yes...?

HEY, SAI...?

That's what I would like to know...

.....

WHY DO YOU THINK YOUR SPIRIT CAME INTO ME? I DON'T EVEN KNOW HOW TO PLAY GO...

MAYBE I CAN TAKE A CLASS OR SOMETHING.

HOW TO PLAY GO...

CLICKETY CLACK

Sigh...

42

COMMUNITY CENTER

EVEN IF WHITE WERE TO PLAY BLACK'S MOVE, BLACK CAPTURES TWO STONES.

...THEN, BLACK DESCENDING HERE IS A GOOD MOVE...

KLAK!

THEN ALL OF WHITE'S STONES IN THIS AREA ARE DEAD.

YAWWWN!!

43

He's going over some basic tsume Go problems-- problems of life and death...

Of course you don't. You're just a beginner.

I DON'T KNOW WHAT THE HECK HE'S TALKING ABOUT...

THAT'S IT FOR MY LECTURE. LET'S START PLAYING SOME GAMES...

A pro...?

HE'S A PRO...

I wonder how good a player this instructor is...

YEAH, HE MAKES A LIVING OFF OF PLAYING GO.

HAVE YOU EVER PLAYED GO, BEFORE?

SKOOT

ONEGAISHIMASU...

CLATTER

YOU MUST BE HIKARU SHINDO...

umm...

NO, I DON'T KNOW A THING ABOUT GO...

SKOOT

ONEGAISHIMASU...*

CLATTER

*Onegaishimasu: a standard greeting to one's opponent before starting a game. Also, literally meaning, "to make a request."

44

OH, I'M NOT REALLY INTERESTED...

WHAT GOT YOU INTERESTED IN GO?

I SEE...

OH, NO... I MEAN--

TEST SCORES?

AFTER ALL, MY TEST SCORES ARE GOING TO IMPROVE AND ALL, SO--

I JUST THOUGHT I SHOULD LEARN THE BASICS.

LET'S START WITH A SIMPLE GAME WHERE WE JUST CAPTURE STONES.

OOPS... MAYBE THAT SOUNDED RUDE...

THAT'S RIGHT. THIS WAY YOU CAN "LEARN THE BASICS."

CAPTURE STONES?

READY...?

.....

IS
HIKARU
HOME?

HELLO!

DING
DONG

WELL,
HELLO
THERE
AKARI!

IS HE
OKAY? DID
SOMETHING
HAPPEN
AGAIN?

NO,
HE'S
NOT...

CREAK

.....

Go...?

lutter
ter

I DON'T
KNOW
WHY HE'S
TAKEN AN
INTEREST
IN IT...

AND HE
ALSO TRIED
TO PLAY GO
WITH HIS
GRAND-
FATHER...

HE'S
STARTED
GOING TO
A WEEKLY
GO
CLASS...

GO?!

46

KLAK!

...NOW, I'LL GO HERE...

OH, NO!

FOR THE REST OF THE HOUR, MAYBE YOU CAN JUST OBSERVE OTHER PEOPLE PLAYING...

I SEE...

I CAPTURE YOUR STONES AND I WIN!

THAT'S TERRIBLE...

PSS PSS

MR. AKOTA'S AT IT AGAIN. PICKING ON A WEAKER PLAYER!

PSS PSS

THERE AREN'T ANY OTHER KIDS HERE...

.....

AHA! *THAT* IS A CRUCIAL MOVE...

Over there. He certainly is not being very nice...

PICKING ON SOME- ONE?

THERE! NOW, I'VE CAPTURED 6 OF YOUR STONES!

KLAK!

YOU SURE DO LIKE GIVING UP YOUR STONES!

But, he's playing a horrible game.

The man who just played. He's a lot better than his opponent...

He's taking advantage of his weaker opponent by being over-aggressive and confusing him.

I-I'M NOT SURE WHAT TO DO...

SLIP

!

NEVER KNOWN ANYONE WHO LIKED LOSING AS MUCH AS YOU SEEM TO!

His play is very mean-spirited!

I will play in his stead!

Trade places with the weaker player!

Hikaru, trade places with his opponent!

I can't take this any more...

HUH?

SAI?

I refuse to stand by and watch a stronger player ridicule a weaker one!

Then, he'll know how it feels to be on the receiving end of such cruel play!

I am going to teach this man a lesson! I'm going to completely overwhelm him...

Hikaru! Don't you believe in my ability?!

BUT, WILL YOUR SKILL FROM 140 YEARS AGO BE ABLE TO COMPETE WITH MODERN PLAYERS FROM THIS AGE?

I UNDER-STAND YOUR PASSION FOR GO...

.....

GRRr!!

When the game has ended, I'm going to give him a piece of my mind! And then, I'm going to--!

CALM DOWN, SAI!

PLIP

AND WE'RE ALL GOING TO HAVE A BIG LAUGH!

I'LL TAKE CARE OF IT!

LEAVE IT TO ME...

OOPS! SORRY!

CRASSSH!

SMIRK!

50

READ THIS WAY

WHAT'S THE BIG IDEA?

clatta clat

I'M SORRY! MY HAND JUST SORT OF SLIPPED...

YOU COMPLETELY RUINED OUR GAME!

STOP!! HEY, WAIT! NO--!

YOU IDIOT! WHAT DO YOU THINK YOU'RE --?!

GRNCH GRNCH

HERE... ALLOW ME... I'LL HAVE IT OFF IN A SEC...

!

KER

ER

PLOP

GACK!!

BUT, I FEEL A LITTLE SORRY FOR HIM...

BUT, IT'S MR. AKOTA WE'RE TALKING ABOUT! HE DESERVED IT!

SNICKER SNICKER

I HAVEN'T LAUGHED THIS MUCH IN A LONG TIME! DID YOU SEE THE LOOK ON MR. AKOTA'S FACE?!

OH MY!

HA HA...

HA HA HA

..... SNICKER SNICKER

OH, DON'T BE TOO HARD ON HIM, SENSEI...

AFTER ALL, I SAW YOU LAUGHING WITH THE REST OF US!

DO YOU UNDERSTAND, HIKARU? I DON'T WANT ANYTHING LIKE THIS TO HAPPEN, EVER AGAIN.

OH, SENSEI...

I UNDERSTAND. EVEN I THINK I WENT TOO FAR...

YEAH...

HIKARU, YOU MUST APOLOGIZE TO MR. AKOTA NEXT WEEK.

HAVE YOU HEARD OF SOMEONE NAMED FUJIWARA-NO-SAI?

UMM...

OH, IT DOESN'T MATTER. FORGET I MENTIONED IT. SEE YOU NEXT WEEK!

NO, I HAVEN'T. DOES THIS PERSON HAVE SOMETHING TO DO WITH GO?

FUJIWARA-NO-SAI...?

I'M NEW HERE, TOO. I STARTED LAST MONTH.

BY THE WAY, SENSEI...

I see...

SENSEI, THAT WAS ANOTHER GREAT CLASS. YOU EXPLAIN EVERYTHING SO CLEARLY!

SO HIKARU, YOU'RE IN THE 6TH GRADE?

UH-HUH...

THANK YOU...

IF WE'RE BOTH NEW, THEN THAT MEANS WE'RE RIVALS!

I GUESS IT DOES!

WELL, I JUST READ AN INTERESTING ARTICLE...

WHO DO YOU THINK'S THE STRONGEST GO PLAYER OF ALL TIME?

See Ya!

"WHO'S THE BEST GO PLAYER TO EVER PLAY THE GAME?"

ON ANOTHER OCCASION, THE REPORTER ASKED A GO PLAYER THE SAME QUESTION.

A REPORTER ASKED A CERTAIN SHOGI* PLAYER THAT QUESTION...

THE SHOGI PLAYER REPLIED THAT, WITHOUT A DOUBT, A PLAYER NAMED HABU WAS THE BEST EVER.

"WHO'S THE BEST SHOGI PLAYER IN HISTORY?"

*a Japanese game similar to Chess   54

AMONGST THE YOUNGER PLAYERS...

KURATA 4 DAN AND OGATA 9 DAN ARE PROBABLY THE BEST

TOYA MEIJIN, WHO HOLDS 3 TITLES, IS CURRENTLY THE BEST PLAYER AROUND.

HON'INBO–SHUSAKU FROM THE EDO PERIOD IS THE BEST PLAYER OF ALL TIME.

BUT AS TO WHO THE BEST *EVER* GO PLAYER THERE WAS--THAT GO PLAYER'S ANSWER WAS UNEQUIVOCALLY CLEAR.

HIKARU AT THE STORY-BOARD STAGE.

Whoa!

OBATA SENSEI DOES THE CHARACTER DESIGNS AND ILLUSTRATIONS FOR THIS MANGA. SO YOU MIGHT BE WONDERING WHAT HAPPENED FOR THE STORYBOARDS BEFORE THE CHARACTERS WERE DESIGNED. WELL, I DREW THEM MYSELF!

HIKARU NO GO
STORYBOARDS ①
YUMI HOTTA

AFTER THAT, I BEGAN TRYING TO IMITATE OBATA SENSEI'S CHARACTER DESIGNS.

I TRIED TO DO IT WITH ALL THE CHARACTERS.

Highlights?

AFTER FINISHING SEVERAL INSTALL-MENTS, I RECEIVED A COPY OF OBATA SENSEI'S FINISHED ARTWORK IN THE MAIL.

I TRY TO IMITATE THE ARTWORK, BUT MINE END UP LOOKING LIKE THIS.

SAI WAS ALSO EASY, VERY SIMILAR TO MY STORYBOARD VERSION.

HIKARU WAS EASY.

I COULDN'T TELL IF I WAS ACTUALLY DOING ANY WORK ON WRITING THE STORY ANYMORE...

IT WAS QUITE FRUS-TRATING!

AKIRA TOYA WAS DIFFICULT. I KEPT DRAWING AND ERASING, DRAWING AND ERASING.

Game 2
"From a
Level Beyond"

WANNA SEE HOW THIS ONE WORKS ...?

Wow! Hmm... A soft drink?

What is this thing?!

IT'S A SOFT DRINK.

"Klank klank thud"?!

HELLO, HIKARU!

Now some sort of orange liquid is coming out!

Gasp! A cup!

WHAT ARE YOU, A CAVEMAN?

.....

YEAH, YEAH...

.....

THAT'S EXACTLY HOW MY GRANDSON IS--ALWAYS DRINKING SODA. IT *CAN'T* BE GOOD FOR YOU...

COMMUNITY CENTER

OH, DEAR WHAT ARE YOU DOING WITH ALL THIS SODA?

HMM?

Hikaru! Something very peculiar is happening in that little box! People are playing Go!

HIKARU, HAVE YOU HEARD OF TOYA MEIJIN? THEY SAY HE'S THE CLOSEST TO HAVING PLAYED "THE DIVINE MOVE."

OH, THE TENGEN MATCH IS ON TV!

I'm a big fan of his!

"THE DIVINE MOVE" ...?

WHITE PLAYS AT P-17, ATTACKING WITH A SMALL KNIGHT'S MOVE.

...BLACK CONNECTS AT R-4...

Another who endeavors to play the Divine Move!

KLAK!

Amazing...

Even during Shusaku's time, there were few who played at such a high level...

His play far exceeds that of a Meijin level...

·····

P A C E

Just a little bit longer!

Please!!

Hikaru, how could you say that?!

HMPH!

HOW BORING!

Mr. Akota...

MR. AKOTA!

?

Oh, come on!

I TOLD YOU, I DON'T WANT TO WATCH THIS ANYMORE!!

UH-OH... I BETTER APOLOGIZE ABOUT LAST WEEK...

·····

Gleam!

HELLO, THERE!

!!

HA HA HA HA!! HAH!

HA HA HA!!

SPLORT!

KIDS THESE DAYS DON'T HAVE ANY MANNERS!

WIPE

HOW RUDE...

WIPE

I COULDN'T HELP IT! YOU SWITCHED WIGS ON ME!

WHAT'S THE BIG IDEA?!

AAAAAGGH!!!

fwoooosh

FWIP!

GASP!

WIPE

SLIP

OKAY, OKAY!!

......!!

You got the teacher mad, and now we can't play Go!

It's all your fault, Hikaru!

SOB SOB

I DIDN'T *MEAN* FOR THIS TO HAPPEN...

DON'T TAKE IT SO HARD, HIKARU. HIRAKAWA SENSEI'S JUST TRYING TO DO WHAT'S BEST FOR YOU...

YOU JUST TRY TO STAY CALM...

I'LL THINK OF SOMETHING...

IT ONLY REALLY STRONG PLAYERS GO THERE. I DON'T THINK YOU'RE READY YET, HIKARU...

IN FRONT OF THE STATION?

THERE'S A GO SALON IN FRONT OF THE TRAIN STATION.

YES, WELL...

HMM?

ARE THERE ANY OTHER PLACES TO PLAY GO AROUND HERE?

Yay!

LET'S GO, SAI!!!

DADUM!!!!

HELLO!

KLAK

KLAK

KLK

KLK

RATTLE

BLOOD DONATION

GO SALON..

GO SALON

OH, THERE IT IS...

I WONDER WHAT IT'LL BE LIKE... I FINALLY GET TO SEE SAI IN ACTION...

GO

66

HM...?

ACTU-ALLY, HE'S A--

SHUF

CAN I PLAY AGAINST HIM?

GREAT! I'M SURE GLAD THERE'S ANOTHER KID HERE! AFTER ALL, IT'S MORE FUN PLAYING AGAINST SOMEONE YOUR OWN AGE!

BUT AKIRA, THIS BOY HAS NEVER--

What?

ARE YOU LOOKING FOR SOME-ONE TO PLAY?

I'LL PLAY YOU...

I'M IN THE 6TH GRADE.

HIKARU SHINDO...

I'M AKIRA TOYA.

LET'S GO BACK THERE.

YOU HAVEN'T PAID YET!

WAIT A MINUTE!

HEY, SO AM I!

THANK YOU!

T-THANKS...

SURE, AKIRA, IF YOU SAY SO. ♡

IT'S HIS FIRST TIME. WHY NOT LET HIM IN FOR FREE?

¥500* FOR YOUTHS.

WHAT?! I HAVE TO PAY?!

*approximately $4.25

¥500...?

Hope I have enough...

68

HOW STRONG A PLAYER ARE YOU?

YOU *THINK* YOU'RE PRETTY GOOD, HUH?

WELL, WHY DON'T YOU PUT DOWN 4 OR 5 STONES FOR NOW.

I DON'T REALLY KNOW, BUT I THINK I'M PRETTY GOOD!

WHO DOES THAT KID THINK HE IS?

NO HANDICAP AGAINST AKIRA TOYA?

ha ha ha

HUH? UMM OKAY, THEN.

AFTER ALL, WE'RE THE SAME AGE!

PUT DOWN 4 OR 5 STONES? I DON'T NEED A HANDICAP.

69

HOWEVER...

HE *IS* "PRETTY GOOD."

HE HOLDS HIS STONES LIKE A BEGINNER, BUT HE PLAYS GOOD SOLID MOVES...

KLAK

KLAK

KLUNK

KLAK

AND WHY DOES HIS HAND STOP SO AWKWARDLY ABOVE THE BOARD...?

THE SHAPE OF HIS *JOSEKI** SEEMS KIND OF OUT-DATED...

*joseki: a standardized set of plays.

!

ACTUALLY...

HE'S NOT INTIMI-DATED BY MY ATTACKS...

NEVER-THE-LESS...

OKAY, 17 UP AND 11 ACROSS...

AH, HERE IT IS...

HAS HE BEEN LEADING THE GAME THIS WHOLE TIME?

HE'S SKILLFULLY COUNTER-ING MY ATTACKS...

KLUNK

IT'S NOT EVEN A GOOD MOVE...

THIS ISN'T THE BEST MOVE...

THIS...

HE'S TESTING MY STRENGTH...

HE PLAYED THERE TO SEE HOW I'LL RESPOND!

FROM A LEVEL WAY BEYOND ME...

HE'S OVER THERE PLAYING WITH A BOY CLOSE TO HIS OWN AGE. AND AKIRA WILL GET MAD IF YOU CALL HIM "SENSEI" AGAIN.

IT'S ONLY RIGHT. AFTER ALL, HE TEACHES ME SO MUCH ABOUT THE GAME...

IS AKIRA SENSEI HERE? I WANTED HIM TO PLAY A TEACHING GAME WITH ME.

WELL, HELLO!

SHLF

BUT HE'S ALREADY GOOD ENOUGH TO PASS... AKIRA SAYS HE WANTS TO WAIT UNTIL HE BECOMES A STRONGER PLAYER.

KLAK

KLAK

I HEAR HE DIDN'T TAKE THE PRO TEST AGAIN THIS YEAR.

FINISHED WITH YOUR GAME?

UH-HUH...

HIS FATHER, TOYA MEIJIN, MUST BE GETTING IMPATIENT WITH HIS SON'S DILLY-DALLY-ING.

74

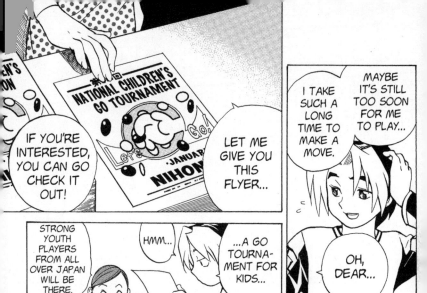

IF YOU'RE INTERESTED, YOU CAN GO CHECK IT OUT!

NATIONAL CHILDREN'S GO TOURNAMENT

LET ME GIVE YOU THIS FLYER...

MAYBE IT'S STILL TOO SOON FOR ME TO PLAY...

I TAKE SUCH A LONG TIME TO MAKE A MOVE.

OH, DEAR...

STRONG YOUTH PLAYERS FROM ALL OVER JAPAN WILL BE THERE.

HMM...

...A GO TOURNAMENT FOR KIDS...

HE'S GOT A LONG WAY TO GO BEFORE HE CAN TAKE ON AKIRA SENSEI.

COME AGAIN!

WELL ANYWAYS, THANKS FOR LETTING ME PLAY TODAY.

HMM? WHAT'S GOING ON IN THERE?

FMP

INTER-ESTING KID, THOUGH...

HMF...

MMBLE

HE LOST...?

MMBLE

MMBLE

MMBLE

*komi – points awarded to white at the end of a game to compensate for black's first move

SKOOT

......!

THAT BOY SAID HE'S NEVER PLAYED A GAME BEFORE!

WAIT A MINUTE!

IS THIS TRUE, AKIRA?! DID YOU REALLY LOSE?

HE'S NEVER PLAYED BEFORE?

HE'S...

Game 3
"Matters of
Life and Death"

OKAY, EVERY-BODY LINE UP!

HIKARU! ARE YOU OKAY?

OKAY, FINE! JUST KEEP QUIET!

I'm sorry! I'm sorry!

HIKARU! EYES FORWARD!

What is that?! A giant bird?!

VWOOOSH

C'MON, SAI! THAT'S JUST AN AIRPLANE!

YOU'RE RIGHT. I HEARD HE EVEN DID THE CORRECTIONS ON HIS SOCIAL STUDIES...

...LIKE HE WAS SUPPOSED TO!

AND NOW HE'S SLACKING OFF IN P.E.!

HIKARU'S BEEN ACTING PRETTY WEIRD LATELY...

.....

PSST!

HEY!

HA HA!

SO YOU SEE, I'VE GOT A LOT OF STUFF GOING ON.

LIKE TAKING GO LESSONS?

GASP!

GASP!

NO WAY!!!

WHAT?! HIKARU'S TAKING GO LESSONS?

HOW DO YOU KNOW ABOUT THAT?

URK!

.....

YOU WOULDN'T BELIEVE HOW BORING AND LAME IT IS!

I CAN'T BELIEVE IT, HIKARU! WHY'RE YOU DOING *THAT*?

ARRGH! DON'T START CRYING AGAIN!

HERE COMES THE TEACH-ER!

Hikaru, how can you say such horrible things? ...Sob sob... Go is not boring!

YOU MAY TAKE YOUR SEATS.

HELLO EVERYONE.

YOU BARELY WON AGAINST THAT 6TH GRADER.

OKAY, EVERYBODY, TIME FOR A TEST.

I EXPECTED YOU TO BE GOOD.

BUT I GUESS YOU'RE NOT THAT GOOD.

I KNOW THAT YOU LOVE GO...

What?

THESE TESTS ARE WARM-UPS FOR YOUR FINALS.

BOO!

WE JUST HAD A SOCIAL STUDIES TEST *LAST* WEEK!

NO!!!

A TEST?!

No, Hikaru, you don't understand. ...sob sob... I was playing a teaching game...

DO YOU KNOW THE ANSWER TO THIS ONE?

HELP ME OUT.

OKAY, SAI.

HISTORY QUESTIONS...

I can't help it. You hate Go. You'll never play unless I do something like this.

江戸幕府Ⅱ

I DIDN'T KNOW YOU WERE LIKE THAT...

YOU'RE TRYING TO MAKE A *DEAL* WITH ME?

SWOOP

If I help you, will you play Go?

HUH?

84

OKAY, FINE. I'LL PLAY GO.

sigh...

.....

HIKARU, WHY HAVEN'T YOU STARTED YET?

Huh?! What? Why?

PLAYING GO IS REALLY TIRING...

NO, WAIT A MINUTE...

RUSTLE

I KNOW WHAT WE CAN DO!

!

85

第19回 NATIONAL CHILDREN'S GO TOURNAMENT

Hmm...

A youth Go tournament...

HERE IT IS...

KRINKLE KRINKLE

THIS WON'T BE SO BAD...

WILL THAT DO?

I'LL TAKE YOU TO THIS...

HIKARU, YOU *STILL* HAVEN'T WRITTEN A WORD...

AAHH!

OKAY, I'M STARTING!

SNICKER SNICKER

HA HA HA HA

CLAP

CLAP

IT MAKES HIM SO HAPPY...

......

日本棋院会館

THE FOLLOWING SUNDAY...

(Japan Go Center)

19TH ANNUAL NATIONAL CHILDREN'S GO TOURNAMENT

WOW!

PRIMARY SCHOOL DIVISION

MIDDLE SCHOOL DIVISION

KLAK

KLAK

KLAK

KLAK

KLAK

KLAK

Incredible!

All these children!

SAI...

THIS IS INCREDIBLE!

And 1000 years from now, there will be more people with this same passion...

There are things I can learn from **them**!

It's the same as my 1000-year-old passion...

These children have the passion...

MAYBE AKIRA TOYA'S HERE...

KLAK

OH, YEAH...

KLAK

Black must make a crucial move in the top left corner or he will die there.

I'LL NEVER FIND HIM...

BUT THERE'S SO MANY PEOPLE HERE...

KLAK KLAK KLAK KLAK KLAK

89

WHERE?

I SEE... HMM... The 2-1 point...

TOO BAD! YOU SHOULD'VE PLAYED ONE POINT HIGHER!

KLAK

OH...

OH! HUH?

OOPS...!

YOU THERE!

GRAB

!

YES...

OGATA SENSEI, I'LL DEAL WITH THIS BOY IN THE OTHER ROOM!

TELL ME WHAT JUST HAPPENED HERE.

SO...

MORI, CALM DOWN!

WHAT'S WRONG WITH YOU?! YOU'RE NOT SUPPOSED TO KIBITZ* IN THE MIDDLE OF A TOURNAMENT MATCH!

UH... I-I'M SORRY!

91

*kibitz - to offer unsolicited advice

HMM, EVEN A PRO MIGHT NOT SEE THIS RIGHT AWAY...

LET'S SEE...

I PLAYED HERE AND THAT KID SAID, "TOO BAD! YOU SHOULD'VE PLAYED ONE POINT HIGHER!"

SO...

IT'S A DIFFICULT SHAPE.

YES, I DID...

...AFTER THE BOY SPOKE OUT, THEN DID YOU UNDERSTAND?

I JUST KIND OF FELT THAT I COULD DO SOMETHING IN THAT AREA...

NO, SIR...

DID YOU RECOGNIZE THAT THIS WAS THE KEY POINT?

AND HOW ABOUT YOU...?

YES...

OGATA SENSEI, THERE'S NO OTHER CHOICE, THEY'LL HAVE TO START A NEW GAME...

THAT'S RIGHT...

AND YOU UNDERSTOOD ONLY AFTER THE OTHER BOY'S COMMENT?

HE DIDN'T HAVE A NAME TAG!

HE DOESN'T EVEN BELONG HERE!

NO, HE ISN'T!

IS THAT BOY A COMPETITOR IN THIS TOURNAMENT?

...THEN HE STOPPED RIGHT BY MY SON'S TABLE...

HE WAS LOOKING AROUND AND WANDERED THIS WAY...

I SAW HIM. HE JUST CAME INTO THE ROOM A FEW MINUTES AGO.

HE GLANCED DOWN AT THE BOARD AND THAT'S WHEN HE DISRUPTED THE GAME!

DID I HEAR YOU CORRECTLY?

"HE *GLANCED* DOWN"?

SOMEONE GOT CAUGHT KIBITZING...

I DON'T THINK HE WAS A PART OF THIS TOURNAMENT...

YOU WOULD THINK THAT ALL THE KIDS IN THIS TOURNAMENT UNDERSTAND HOW BAD IT IS TO KIBITZ.

MUST'VE BEEN THAT KID THEY JUST ESCORTED OUT OF HERE...

HIS COMMENT COULD'VE BEEN CORRECT OUT OF PURE DUMB LUCK.

......

I DIDN'T SEE THE BOARD SO I DON'T REALLY KNOW.

BUT IF HE CAN COMMENT ON A GAME, HE MUST KNOW SOMETHING ABOUT GO...

THE 3RD ROUND OF THE MIDDLE SCHOOL DIVISION IS ABOUT TO BEGIN.

THE OTHERS ARE STILL PLAYING THEIR GAMES.

KLAK

QUIET PLEASE...

KLAK

KLAK

Japan Go

全国こども囲

中学生の部

優勝

95　(National Children's Go)

HA HA HA!

THESE PLAYERS TAKE THIS TOURNAMENT VERY SERIOUSLY.

THIS *IS* A VERY SERIOUS MATTER, YOUNG MAN.

YOU'RE RIGHT. OF COURSE NOT! I'M VERY SORRY.

THIS IS NO LAUGHING MATTER!

SORRY I CAUSED SO MUCH TROUBLE!

I SUPPOSE SO...

THAT'LL DO, WON'T IT, KAKIMOTO SENSEI?

WELL, WHY DON'T YOU LEAVE FROM THE REAR EXIT.

96

HMM...

SO WHAT WAS THE PLAY THAT BOY COMMENTED ON?

THIS MUST BE A FIRST.

MY GOODNESS...

I feel bad for those two boys...

I FEEL BAD... MY MOUTH JUST WENT ON AUTO-PILOT.

E-EXCUSE ME...

OOPS...

B U M P

OUCH!

I'VE HAD JUST ABOUT ENOUGH OF THIS GAME.

mutter mutter

I DON'T THINK I'M MUCH SUITED FOR IT.

FWUMP

PHEW! I THOUGHT HE WAS GOING TO YELL AT ME!

RIGHT, SAI?

.....

CAREFUL NOW...

UH...

SAI...?

?

He, too, endeavors to play the *Divine Move!*

That man...

I've seen him before...

TAKE A LOOK AT THIS!

I UNDER-STAND THERE WAS SOME TROUBLE.

K L K

CREAK

TOYA MEIJIN...

MMBL

MM

A YOUNG MAN COMMENTED ON THIS. IT MIGHT EVEN TAKE A PRO SOME TIME TO SEE THE PROPER PLAY...

BUT HE ONLY *GLANCED* AT THE BOARD.

I DIDN'T KNOW THERE WERE ANY CHILDREN OTHER THAN MY SON AKIRA WHO COULD DO SUCH A THING.

HE IMMEDIATELY RECOGNIZED THE KEY POINT...

I SEE...

SHUF

NO MATTER...

S-SORRY...

AND *THEY* LET HIM GO WITHOUT EVEN GETTING HIS NAME...

GAME 4 "Inexcusable"

AND THIS MOVE, TOO...

THIS MOVE...

COULD HE REALLY BE THAT STRONG?

IT'S AS IF HE WAS PLAYING A TEACHING GAME.

WHO **WAS** THAT KID?

I JUST DON'T UNDER-STAND.

THERE'S NO WAY A KID COULD BE **THAT** GOOD.

NO, THERE'S NO WAY...

AKIRA...?

HIKARU SHINDO!

I'M... SORRY...

......

IT'S OKAY IF YOU DON'T FEEL LIKE IT...

MR. HIROSE WANTED YOU TO PLAY A TEACHING GAME WITH HIM...

I GUESS ALL YOU CAN DO IS WAIT FOR HIM TO COME BACK.

WE DON'T KNOW ANYTHING ABOUT THAT BOY EXCEPT HIS NAME.

......

......

.....

THAT'S RIGHT. HE DIDN'T SEEM VERY INTERESTED, BUT MAYBE HE WENT ANYWAY.

THE ONE AT THE GO ASSOCIATION?

BEFORE HE LEFT, I GAVE HIM A FLYER FOR THE YOUTH GO TOURNAMENT.

WAIT A MINUTE

SKOOT

AKIRA?!

SLAM

OH...

IF HE COMES HERE...

PLEASE HAVE HIM WAIT UNTIL I COME BACK.

OF COURSE HE'S CHANGING.

AKIRA SURE HAS CHANGED...

BEFORE NOW, THERE'S NEVER BEEN ANYONE AROUND WHOM HE COULD CONSIDER A RIVAL.

DASH

I CAN'T DENY IT...

ULP!

You were trying to show off!

And I was having such a good time watching all the children play.

Sob.

SNIFF

SNIFF

ARRGH! SHUT UP ALREADY!

It's all your fault, Hikaru! All your fault! All your fault! All your fault!

I'm not the one with the big mouth, Hikaru. *You* are!

GRRR!

SAI, NONE OF THIS WOULD'VE HAPPENED IF YOU HADN'T OPENED YOUR BIG MOUTH!!

SOB!

ARRGGH!!

Sob sob!

108

UM...

AKIRA TOYA!

WHAT'RE *YOU* DOING HERE?

VWOO... OOOOSH

SHUF

WEREN'T YOU PLAYING IN THE YOUTH GO TOURNAMENT?

.....

NO, I JUST TOOK A QUICK LOOK IN THERE...

ME?

WERE *YOU* PLAYING IN IT?

THERE WERE LITTLE KIDS YOUNGER THAN ME IN THERE, AND THEY WERE ALL SO INTENSE.

BUT YOU KNOW WHAT?

IT WAS REALLY SOMETHING.

WHAT'S UP WITH *HIM?*

.....

110

One doesn't play Go solely for the sake of monetary rewards!

WHAT DO YOU SAY?

WELL?

SAI, THINK YOU'RE GOOD ENOUGH TO GET THE MEIJIN TITLE?

¥100,000,000

WOW!!!

MAYBE IT WOULDN'T BE SO BAD!

No, Hikaru!! That is *not* what Go is all about!

No!

I DIDN'T KNOW YOU GET RICH FROM PLAYING GO!

flap flap

"DABBLE AROUND AND BECOME A PRO?"
"WIN A TITLE OR TWO?"

WIN A TITLE OR TWO, HERE AND THERE...

WOULDN'T BE SO BAD?

DABBLE AROUND AND BECOME A PRO...

YEAH, YOU KNOW...

I, UH...

HUH?

YOU'VE JUST OFFENDED EVERY PROFESSIONAL GO PLAYER OUT THERE...

THOSE WORDS...

SHUF

HIS HANDS DON'T BEAR THE MARKS OF A GO PLAYER AND HE HOLDS HIS STONES LIKE A BEGINNER...

YOU'RE NO GO PLAYER. ANYONE WHO REALLY PLAYS THE GAME WOULD NEVER SAY ANYTHING SO INEXCUSABLE!

Sigh...

D-DID I SAY SOMETHING WRONG?

I UNDERESTI-MATED HIM BECAUSE I THOUGHT HE WAS A BEGINNER, THEN I PAN-ICKED AND DESTROYED MYSELF.

HOW?! HOW COULD I HAVE LOST TO *HIM?* MAYBE I UNDERESTI-MATED HIM AND LET DOWN MY GUARD...

I, TOO, HAVE WORKED HARD AND MADE SACRI-FICES...

I'VE PLAYED HOURS AND HOURS OF GO EVERY DAY SINCE I WAS A LITTLE KID. I'VE WORKED SO HARD...

CLENCH

HUH?

LET'S PLAY A GAME RIGHT NOW.

And it's all your fault!!

GRRR!!

Hikaru! We hardly spent any time at the Go tour-nament!

YIKES! OKAY, OKAY!

HIKARU

I THINK I'VE ALREADY HAD MY FILL OF GO FOR TODAY...

RIGHT NOW?

Game 5
"Akira Bares His Fangs"

KLANK

KLANK

VWOOSH

mutter mutter

IF BLACK MOVES THERE, THEN WHITE SHOULD...

......

JEEZ! CAN'T HE TAKE A JOKE?

NOW AKIRA'S REALLY MAD...

I DIDN'T MEAN IT WHEN I SAID I'D BECOME A PRO AND WIN A TITLE OR TWO...

I WAS JUST KIDDING AROUND.

OH BOY...

ARGH! CAN'T ANYONE TAKE A JOKE AROUND HERE?

A joke? Are you sure you were just kidding?

C'MON, SAI!

LAST TIME, YOU ONLY BEAT AKIRA BY 2 POINTS.

WHAT DO YOU TAKE ME FOR?

I KNOW IT WOULDN'T BE THAT EASY FOR YOU TO BECOME A PRO...

That was a teaching game.

I wouldn't try so hard against a child.

WHAT?

Hikaru, I wasn't actually trying to win that game.

Words are not needed. The moves do all the talking.

One does not play to win. Nothing is learned if the instructor has an overwhelming victory.

A TEACHING GAME?

The goal of a teaching game is to guide the other player to make the correct moves.

VWSH

HMM... SO YOU *ARE* BETTER THAN AKIRA...

Did you say Akira is "just a kid"?

What was that, Hikaru?

OF COURSE YOU'RE BETTER THAN HIM.

SO WHAT? HE'S JUST A KID IN THE 6TH GRADE, JUST LIKE ME.

Only the most skilled of players would be able to beat him.

Although he still has room to grow, his moves are superb.

When this child reaches his full potential...

With every move he makes, I can feel his talent awakening...

Akira is far from being "just a kid."

...Or perhaps a dragon...

He will transform into a lion...

GASP!

KLAK

KLAK

KLAK

AKIRA!

I'M GOING TO USE THE TABLE IN THE BACK.

SHUF

CLATTER

THE ONE THAT BEAT AKIRA?

IT'S HIM!

CLATTER

THAT'S RIGHT, THAT'S HIM!

HEY!

GASP!

HE'S THE ONE!

MMBL

THAT BOY...

MMBL

FWUUMM

.....

MMBL

W-WAIT A MINUTE...

MMBL

HAVE A SEAT.

That's what I've been trying to tell you!

HE'S NOT JUST SOME KID...

THIS CROWD'S NOT AFFECTING HIM ONE BIT...

HE'S NOT EVEN CONSCIOUS OF THE SURROUNDINGS.

How should this situation be handled?

Now then...

This is a delicate time in his development...

Should I be gentle with him...?

But right now he is baring his teeth.

This child is bright-eyed and overflowing with potential...

Komi?

KOMI?

THE KOMI COUNTS FOR 5 1/2 POINTS.

ALL RIGHT! I GOT IT! I'M BLACK!

LET'S SEE... TWO, FOUR, SIX... TWELVE. IT'S EVEN.

SO TO COMPENSATE, WHITE GETS 5 1/2 POINTS.

BY GOING FIRST, BLACK HAS THE ADVANTAGE.

SHUFFLE SHUFFLE

DIDN'T YOU KNOW ABOUT THIS, SAI?

What? By 5 1/2 points?

IF THE END SCORE IS 50 TO 50, THEN WHITE WINS BY 5 1/2 POINTS.

YOU NEVER THOUGHT THAT WAS UNFAIR?

I've never lost while playing black.

burn

DIDN'T YOU EVER THINK THAT BLACK HAD AN ADVANTAGE?

This rule did not exist in Hon'inbo-Shusaku's time...

134

The 3-4 point nearest you in the upper right-hand corner.

KLUNK

KLAK

SHUF

Now the 3-4 point nearest you in the lower right-hand corner.

TUNK

AKIRA TOOK 3 MINUTES TO MAKE HIS FIRST MOVE...

KLAK

HE'S REALLY MAD...

AKIRA'S GOT A SCARY LOOK IN HIS EYES...

Perhaps the pincer would be more effective...

Playing the diagonal on the next move may be a bit too timid...

Or is he *waiting* for me to play the diagonal?

hmm...

Well then, I'll just have to comply...

GLARE!!

The diag-onal.

Next, play 16-15...

Now...

KLK

HIKARU
NO GO
EXTRAS

Hikaru
no Go
Q&A

Q 1 Is it true that there are smaller Go boards?

A A standard Go board, such as the one shown to the right, has 19 by 19 points. This may be too large an area and may cause confusion for beginners. So instead, a 9 by 9 board can be used.

A 19 by 19 Go board with legs typically used by the pros.

Q 2 What kind of person was Hon'inbo-Shusaku?

A Shusaku was a genius Go player born in 1829 in Innoshima. He had such great skill that some called him the greatest player of all time. He learned the game at age 5 and by the time he was 10, he was playing Go in Edo, the capital city. It is said that his master, Jowa, called Shusaku a great player the likes of which had not been seen in 150 years. Shusaku eventually developed into such an outstanding player, he came to be known as a "Go Saint."

KLAK

Hikaru, are you ready?

SHUF

Game 6: "A Decisive Blow"

Game 6
"A Decisive Blow"

FSHHH

TICK

TOCK

TICK

I RESIGN...

.....

SHUF

HUH?!

WHAT--?!

BUT--?!

WAIT A MINUTE...

SHUF

He's admitted that he cannot win this game.

Akira conceded defeat.

WHAT JUST HAPPENED?!

SHUF

I MEAN... WE'VE PLAYED LESS THAN HALF OF WHAT WE DID BEFORE...

I-I DON'T KNOW WHAT'S GOING ON...

...AKIRA...

.....

SAI...

...DID YOU REALLY JUST BEAT THE PANTS OFF HIM...?

YOU REALLY PUT THE PRESSURE ON ME WITH EVERY ONE OF YOUR MOVES!

I'M REALLY IMPRESSED WITH YOUR INTENSITY...

Y-YOU'RE REALLY SOMETHING, AKIRA...

SKOOT

YOU... REALLY WERE... GREAT...

HE'S NOT LISTENING TO ME...

THOSE GUYS AT THE TOURN-AMENT HAD NOTHING ON YOU!

SEE YA...

I-I'M GOING HOME...

DOESN'T HEAR A WORD I SAY...

HE CAN'T HEAR ME AT ALL...

FATHER... FATHER...

YOU HAVE TWO FACTORS IN YOUR FAVOR...

BUT I DO KNOW THIS...

WELL, I CAN'T SAY FOR SURE...

GOOD AT GO...?

DO YOU THINK I'LL EVER BE ANY GOOD AT GO?

HAVE YOU HEARD A SINGLE WORD I'VE SAID?

HEY!

.....

.....

Tp Tp

SHE CHASED AFTER THE STRAY CAT THAT STOLE OUR FISH!

...AND MY MOM IS SO SILLY...

...INTENSITY...

INTENSITY...

.....

I THOUGHT YOU WERE JUST GOING TO WIN BY 2 POINTS AGAIN...

SAI...?

WHY'D YOU HAVE TO WIN LIKE *THAT*, SAI?

I'VE NEVER SEEN...

WHERE'RE YOU GOING? THIS IS THE WAY HOME...

I'M NOT GOING HOME...

NAW, NO GO CLASS TODAY...

ARE YOU GOING TO THAT GO CLASS OF YOURS?

WHY'RE YOU ACTING SO WEIRD, HIKARU?!

GEEZ!

GO SALON

AM 9:00 ～ 12:00
PM 2:00 ～ 5:00

P.E.O.T.W

IS GO MORE THAN JUST A GAME...?

ARE YOU TRYING TO PLAY "THE DIVINE MOVE" JUST LIKE SAI...?

AKIRA, HOW CAN YOU BE SO INTENSE...?

Then why did you come all this way?!

I SAID FORGET IT!

I'M JUST NOT IN THE MOOD, OKAY?

TP

Hikaru, are we going to play Go again today?!

Oh, come now!

FORGET IT!

154

HEY!

WHAT'S THE BIG IDEA?!

IT *IS* YOU!

WHAT'RE YOU--?!

FWOOM

OUCH! HEY, SLOW DOWN!

MEIJIN!

THERE'S SOMEONE WHO'S BEEN WANTING TO MEET YOU...

COME WITH ME...

GO SALON

HUH?! WHO?

IS IT AKIRA TOYA?

TP TP TP

◄◄ READ THIS WAY ◄◄

I THINK I'VE SEEN HIM BEFORE...

AKIRA'S FATHER?

TOYA?

TOYA... MEIJIN?

KLAK

"THE DIVINE MOVE" GUY!

OH MY GOSH! IT'S *HIM*!

P.E.O... GO

...BUT TWICE...

...NOT ONCE...

KLAK

SO THAT'S THE BOY WHO BEAT AKIRA...

.....

HM...

GASP!

Hikaru!

FINE, I'LL PLAY...

SKOOT

THAT'S HOW GOOD AKIRA IS.

THREE STONES AGAINST THE HOLDER OF THE MEIJIN TITLE. DO YOU KNOW WHAT THAT MEANS?

THAT'S HOW I PLAY WITH AKIRA...

PUT DOWN THREE STONES.

» READ THIS WAY «

THIS MAN HAS AKIRA'S SAME INTENSITY...

KLUNK

HMPH...

I'M THE ONLY ONE WHO DOESN'T BELONG...

.....

I BET SAI HAS IT TOO...

I WANT TO...

LET'S BEGIN...

SAI, I WANT TO...

KL AK

Hikaru...

.....

P.E.O.T.W

GASP!

Approach at 3-5!

OKAY, 3-5...

KLUNK

.....

Attach at 3-3...

WOW!

KLAK

BUT THIS GUY HAS STYLE TOO...

I THOUGHT THE WAY AKIRA PLACES HIS STONES ON THE BOARD WAS COOL...

KLUNK

I'VE BEEN TEACHING AKIRA GO SINCE HE WAS TWO YEARS OLD.

!

KLAK

AKIRA IS ON A DIFFERENT LEVEL.

IF HE WERE TO PLAY IN A YOUTH TOURNAMENT, HE WOULD CRUSH THE HOPES OF ANY ASPIRING PLAYERS.

Play the 4-4 star point.

I DON'T ALLOW HIM TO PLAY IN AMATEUR TOURNAMENTS.

KLUNK

KLAK

WE PLAY A GAME EVERY MORNING. HE'S GOOD ENOUGH TO BE A PRO.

163

IT ALMOST LOOKS LIKE HIS FINGER-TIPS ARE GLOWING!

WOW!

P.E.O.T.W GO

HE TAKES THE STONE IN BETWEEN PLIANT FINGERS...

AND RELEASES THE STONE ABOVE THE BOARD.

Now descend at 2-3.

THAT IS WHY...

KLUNK

THAT IS WHY IT IS DIFFICULT FOR ME TO BELIEVE...

FWISH

I..I WANT TO BE ABLE TO DO THAT...

The 16-10 star point.

HIS FINGER-TIPS ARE GLOWING!

...THAT SOME CHILD DEFEATED AKIRA.

P.E.O.T.

SHUF

KLA

Hikaru no Go Q&A

Q **3** **You win Shogi (Japanese Chess) by capturing the king. How do you win Go?**

A The winner of Go is the side, White or Black, that has more territory. In the figure shown, Black's territory is on the right, White's territory is on the left. Which side is the winner?

Territory is counted by number of points. In this diagram, Black has 26 points and White has 29 points. White wins by 3 points.

Q **4** **Can anyone go to a Go Salon?**

A Yes, go ahead and go to one if you see one in town. The people there are sure to welcome children, women, and anyone new to Go.

Q **5** **How old do you have to be to become a pro?**

A Go is strictly a world of ability. Anyone can become a pro as long as they pass the test to qualify, even a small child. Of course, it's not easy. Cho Chi-hoon (known in Japan as Cho Chikun) became a pro at the young age of 11.

Q **6** **My school doesn't have a Go club. How can I start playing?**

A One way is to learn from Go on TV and from books, but maybe someone you know plays Go – your father, an uncle, or maybe one of your teachers at school. If you can't think of anyone, try going to a Go salon. There's also plenty of Go classes for kids at community centers. You can get more details by contacting the American Go Association at www.usgo.org.

Game 7: "Three Problems of Life and Death"

Game 7
"Three Problems
of Life and Death"

CLATTER!!

HMM...

WHAT HAP- PENED...?

HOW WAS HE...?

HOW...

I GUESS IT WAS MY FAULT. I FORCED HIM HERE...

SHUF

.....

171

SO HE IS--

AS GOOD AS A PRO...

THERE WAS NOTHING WRONG WITH HIS PLAY. HE HAD GOOD SOLID MOVES.

I SEE...

I COULDN'T TELL HOW STRONG A PLAYER HE IS.

BUT I ONLY SAW HIM MAKE A FEW PLAYS.

MOST WOULD CONSIDER IT TO BE A BAD MOVE...

HOW-EVER...

IT WAS INDEED VERY INTERESTING...

YES...?

HOW-EVER...

THE LAST MOVE HE MADE WAS QUITE INTER-ESTING...

IT'S NO-THING.

172

YOU TOOK CONTROL OF MY BODY, DIDN'T YOU?!

DARN IT, SAI!!

MY SOUL WASN'T ENOUGH! YOU HAD TO TAKE OVER MY BODY TOO!

I CAN'T PLACE A STONE DOWN LIKE THAT!!

ARE YOU LIS- TENING TO ME?!

VWOOSH

FWOOSH

ARR!

GRR!

DON'T STARE AT HIM!

TP TP TP

THEN YOU'RE SAYING I PUT THAT STONE DOWN ALL ON MY OWN?!

Yes! Yes! That's right!

P.E. O.T.W

You're wrong, Hikaru! I can do no such thing!

Yes! Try snapping this rock down!

THIS ROCK?

Hikaru! Try this rock!

STOP LYING! HOW COULD I HAVE DONE THAT?!

PLIP

FP

SLIP

P.E.O.T.W G !

DARN IT...

FP

HEY! I THINK I GOT IT!

DON'T TRY TO TRAIN ME LIKE SOME KIND OF CIRCUS MONKEY! I'LL--

SHUT UP!

Hikaru, try it with your fingers more--

I TOLD YOU! I CAN'T DO IT!!

NOW I JUST SMACK IT DOWN!!

ALL RIGHT!!!

SKRNCH

BUT...

YOU'VE GOT A POINT...

But, Hikaru, you really played that stone on your own. You didn't even put it down where I told you to!

HMM...

Fine... Go ahead and think that if you want...

fwip

I LET MY GUARD DOWN AND YOU TOOK OVER MY BODY!!

You are becoming more familiar with the game and I think you want to start playing on your own...

But, Hikaru, *you* really did make that move...

AKIRA'S BEEN LEARNING FROM HIS FATHER FOR A LONG TIME...

BUT TOYA MEIJIN SURE DOES PLAY WITH A LOT OF STYLE.

He just snaps the stone down...

Hikaru, it's really not that difficult.

Hmph!

AND I CAN'T EVEN HOLD THE STONE RIGHT...

HIKARU!

HEY...

FORGET IT!!

I can't do it...

Come on, try it one more time!

Where'd that rock go?

I'LL MEET YOU AT THE FRONT GATE OF HAZE MIDDLE SCHOOL THIS SUNDAY AT 2 O'CLOCK.

LET'S GO...

I'M NOT GOING.

THAT'S OKAY...

NAW...

WHY NOT? WE GET TO EAT TAKOYAKI* FOR FREE!

*octopus batter balls.

I'M KINDA HUNGRY. MAYBE I'LL GET SOME RAMEN...

.....

SHUT UP, SAI! DO YOU WANT TO DIE?

...

I think that girl likes you.

I already am dead.

BE THERE AT 2 O'CLOCK!

FORGET IT. IF ANYONE SEES ME WALKING AROUND WITH A GIRL, I'LL NEVER HEAR THE END OF IT.

Why don't you go, Hikaru?

Hey! Look over there!

I see...

DIFFERENT CLUBS FROM THE SCHOOL PUT UP BOOTHS.

SOMETHING LIKE THAT.

Look, Hikaru! ♡

OKAY, OKAY... WE'LL GO TAKE A LOOK.

HERE'S AN INTERMEDIATE PROBLEM.

They're playing Go!!

SOLVE THE PROBLEM IN THREE MOVES.

KLK

...HERE.

FIRST BLACK ATTACHES HERE...

THEN WHITE GOES...

SCOOT

THIS IS PRETTY HARD...

OH, I SEE...

WHAT IF WHITE GOES HERE?

KLK

PROBLEMS OF LIFE AND DEATH BY TOYA MEIJIN

Hikaru, what's that book?

IT'S THE GRAND PRIZE!

SHUF

SHUF

"PROBLEMS OF LIFE AND DEATH" BY TOYA MEIJIN...

SURE.

CAN I TRY?

KLATTER

UGH! ER...

Hikaru! I want it! I want it!

SAI, LET *ME* SOLVE IT...

HEY, I THINK EVEN I CAN GET THIS ONE.

OKAY...

TRY THIS...

CLAP

YOU TOOK A LOT OF TIME, BUT YOU GOT IT!

YOU DID IT!

WOW!!

NOT BAD!

CLAP CLAP

CLAP

.....

IS THAT RIGHT?

KLUNK

KLUNK

KLUNK

When you get a bit more familiar with Go like Hikaru, you, too, will be able to see that White was dead after the third move.

White succeeded in capturing Black with 10, but now if Black plays the center point, he will capture all of White's stones.

Black plays inside again. White captures the invading stone.

With 6, White captures all of Black's invading stones.

Black goes inside to kill White. White attempts to surround Black's invading stones.

How can Black kill all of White's stones?

Hikaru is still a beginner, but he was able to solve this problem because he is learning the fundamentals in his Go class. Here's an explanation of the problem Hikaru solved. (The numbers indicate the order of play.)

Sai's Commentary

Otherwise, we won't get the book!

Hikaru, you have to solve a harder one than that!

TWITCH TWITCH

WHA--?!

TISSUE?!

WHAT ABOUT THE BOOK?!

HERE'S YOUR PRIZE.

ARE YOU SURE?

A HARDER ONE?

SHF SHF SHF

UMM... GIVE ME A HARDER ONE...

HUH?!

GASP!

14-3, 14-4, and 16-1!!

THIS ONE'S FOR A DAN LEVEL PLAYER. EVEN I'D HAVE TROUBLE WITH THIS ONE.

SOLVE IT IN THREE MOVES.

KLNK KLNK KLNK

Y-YOU GOT IT...

.....

LET'S HURRY UP AND GET THIS OVER WITH...

I WANT TO WIN THE GO BOOK! GIVE ME THE HARDEST ONE YOU GOT!

INSTANTANEOUS...

THAT WAS QUICK...

.....

WHAT?! SODA...?

THIS NEXT ONE'S AKIRA TOYA LEVEL...

THE HARDEST ONE...?

AND HE PLAYS TEACHING GAMES FOR ADULTS...

THEY SAY HE'S GOOD ENOUGH TO BE A PRO.

SCOOT

I KNOW THAT GUY. IS HE REALLY THAT GOOD?!

AKIRA TOYA?!

READ THIS WAY

AKIRA TOYA *MIGHT* BE ABLE TO SOLVE THIS PROBLEM.

I'VE SEEN HIM WHEN HE'S PLAYING A GAME.

THE FIRST MOVE IS THE KEY.

THERE YOU GO.

HE'S SO INTENSE, IT'S SCARY.

HERE GOES...

AKIRA WOULD BE ABLE TO SOLVE THIS ONE, HUH?

chew chew

FWOOM

SQUISH

...RIGHT HERE!

PLAY YOUR FIRST MOVE...

SCOOT

WHAT'S THE BIG IDEA?!

IT'S FOR LOSERS.

FORGET ABOUT THIS LAME GAME.

!!

GASP!

SQUISH

SQUISH

Next Volume Preview

It's tournament time—and the Haze and Kaio Middle School Go Clubs are both contenders for an ultimate championship that will entail months of practice and turmoil among its finest players.

So it begins, with an in-your-face challenge from Tetsuo Kaga to Hikaru Shindo. If go stones could talk, White and Black would be up in arms picketing for the fair treatment of game pieces. Meanwhile, teams are being methodically organized for maximum match victories.

While Akira joins Kaio Middle School as their star go-playing phenom, Hikaru has been playing for Haze Middle School's Go Team—to satisfy Sai's appetite for go and his own burgeoning curiosity for the game. Still, Hikaru remains a dark cloud over Akira's game. Someday soon, they will play each other again to defend their schools, their teams, their reputations and, finally, their own passions for this ancient game.

AVAILABLE NOW

You're Reading in the Wrong Direction!!

Whoops! Guess what? You're starting at the wrong end of the comic!

…It's true! In keeping with the original Japanese format, **Hikaru no Go** is meant to be read from right to left, starting in the upper-right corner.

Unlike English, which is read from left to right, Japanese is read from right to left, meaning that action, sound effects and word-balloon order are completely reversed… something which can make readers unfamiliar with Japanese feel pretty backwards themselves. For this reason, manga or Japanese comics published in the U.S. in English have sometimes been published "flopped"—that is, printed in exact reverse order, as though seen from the other side of a mirror.

By flopping pages, U.S. publishers can avoid confusing readers, but the compromise is not without its downside. For one thing, a character in a flopped manga series who once wore in the original Japanese version a T-shirt emblazoned with "M A Y" (as in "the merry month of") now wears one which reads "Y A M"! Additionally, many manga creators in Japan are themselves unhappy with the process, as some feel the mirror-imaging of their art skews their original intentions.

We are proud to bring you Yumi Hotta and Takeshi Obata's **Hikaru no Go** in the original unflopped format. For now, though, turn to the other side of the book and let the adventure begin…!

—Editor

5050 3300 347293

J
HOT